Jill M. Hudson

Evaluating Ministry

Principles and

Processes for

Clergy and

Congregations

AN ALBAN INSTITUTE PUBLICATION

Library of Congress Catalog Card #91-78151
ISBN   1-56699-054-6

CONTENTS

I. Why Evaluate?   1

II. Grounded in Theology   6

III. Pitfalls and Potholes   10

IV. We Did It!   15

V. Denominations Can Help   58

VI. A Dozen Reminders   64

Notes   69

Bibliography   73

CHAPTER I

Why Evaluate?

"Our pastor shouldn't use so many illustrations from novels; I wish he'd just preach the Bible!". . . . "That was a terrific steward-ship dinner. I wondered who planned the program?". . . "I can't believe only six people showed for the Lenten study—everyone said they wanted one. The vestry promised me if I prepared there would be fifty!" . . . "If she'd just look me in the eye when we shake hands after church services I'd feel so much better. I don't think she likes me at all. I thought women in ministry were sup-posed to be so caring and warm. What a disappointment!" . . . "My parishioners expect me to do all the work. They think I'm the paid Christian around here!"

Sound familiar? Evaluation is a daily occurrence in the life of the parish. It happens in the parking lot, over the telephone, in the manse. Reflecting on how the pastor is doing, how the Sunday school teachers are doing, how the "church" is doing is part of what it means to be thoughtful, conscientious, caring people. Most of us take seriously our roles as members, leaders, or pastors of congregations. We are constantly struggling with whether or not we're being faithful to God's calling. Yet the idea of *formal* evaluation is often resisted—a scary and threatening idea for church professionals and lay leaders alike. We generally associate "evaluation" with "judgment," and no one likes to be judged! Often congregations don't conduct evaluations, believing that "no news is good news." Perhaps they are afraid of learning things that may demand change or open a Pandora's box. Evaluations take time—a valuable commodity in busy churches. Why not leave well enough alone? Pastors often fear that evaluations will reveal painful critiques of their leadership, or—even worse—be used to orchestrate their departure. These fears are, unfortunately, too often founded in reality. There are many cases when evaluation has been used as a weapon against a pastor or where review led to greater frustration for lay leaders instead of new energy for ministry. The purpose of this book is to explore ways of conducting ministry evaluation that can be healthy, life-enhancing, and supportive of the gifts and talents of all who are engaged in the mission of a particular congregation. But first we need to answer the question: If this produces so much anxiety, why do it at all?

The Purpose of Evaluation

"The purpose of evaluation is not to prove but to improve."[1] This quote from the flyleaf of the Phi Delta Kappa book states positively the goal of evaluation. Evaluation can be considered an ongoing process that strengthens our ministry, giving us the opportunity to reflect periodically on how well we are fulfilling our commitments to Christ, the church, and one another. It helps both clergy and laity redefine their current sense of calling and identify where they are feeling good about their ministry, what may need more attention, and what can appropriately be "put to rest" as no longer needed. In his helpful pamphlet "Evaluation of, by, for and to the Clergy," Loren Mead reminds us that the work of ministry is "that task in which pastors and laity collaborate to press each other and nurture each other into growth within their religious tradition, that task that produces people who go into their worlds to try to make a difference for others and for that world."[2] Surely this task is worthy of review and conversation!

The Importance of Mutual Evaluation

> Excellence in ministry is not a one-person show. Even
> with vigorous and dynamic pastoral leadership, long-term
> excellence in faithfully carrying out the mission of the
> Gospel occurs only where the laity are committed to the
> vision of what their congregation's ministry can be. In the
> excellent churches, the laity own, take responsibility for,
> and are trusted with carrying out the work of the people of
> God.[3]

This quote from *Pursuing Excellence in Ministry* points to the
essential partnership of clergy and laity in executing the ministry
of a congregation. Central to this book is the belief that evaluating
only the pastor's performance results in denying the laity the
growth and empowerment that can come from meaningful review.

Richard Ullman, Archdeacon of the Episcopal Diocese of
Southern Ohio, makes this point in his article "Taking Stock of
Our Ministry" when he states, "Paul wrote that 'we, though many,
are one body in Christ, and individually members one of another'
(Romans 12:5). Ministry is and must be mutual. Therefore, no
individual's performance in ministry can be reviewed with fairness
apart from the whole. To look at the pastor's performance in
isolation from that of the other key ministers in the congregation
(e.g. the members) encourages defensive, win-lose behavior and
feelings."[4] To separate the ministry of one Christian, namely the
pastor, for evaluation without considering the ministry of those
with whom he or she shares the work of a particular congregation
is not only unjust but theologically unsound! There are particular
times when a pastor may request a comprehensive review of his or
her own ministry for growth or personal assessment. The models
in Chapter Four will consider both a mutual review and those times
when a pastor, on his or her own initiative, makes the request to
evaluate his or her ministry alone.

Anticipated Outcomes of Evaluation

There are three large payoffs for congregations and pastors willing to engage in mutual assessment.

1) New realizations will emerge. Whatever methods are used in the review process, surprises will surely occur. Areas of ministry that have felt troubled or uncertain may yield the key to the puzzle. Dynamics of parish life that were thought to be going well may reveal areas of concern. What are we doing better than we thought? Where do we need improvement? There will be unexpected success and honest feedback. Even the long standing successes may help us discover new insights.

2) New goals and directions can be established. The process of examining current ministry can lead us to the development of new priorities. Where are the emerging needs of our congregation, potential outreach, and service in our community? This also involves weighing what needs to be lovingly brought to conclusion in order to make room for the unfolding areas of future ministry.

3) The mysterious relationship between pastor and members will be explored. It is impossible for a congregation to review ministry without looking at how they are living together as pastor and people. The deep psychological dimensions of religious identity surface in traditional imagery of the minister as shepherd, of members as the fold, of both as the community of faith. Such metaphors weave themselves in and out of the review process. Don Hagerty, a Presbyterian pastor in Chicago, wrote of this in an article for *The Christian Century* several years ago when he suggested that a review gets into the subtle nuances of the pastor-church relationship that go beyond whether a particular pastor is liked or viewed as effective. He says, "The issue is more of relativities, adjustments, emphases and gentle shifts."[5] Although we often try to legislate changes around these areas, a thoughtful review process may simply allow the recognition that few relationships are without room to grow. Being able to talk about these in the context of mutual love and respect can be a liberating and healing occurrence.

In Summary

A pastor and congregation who are willing to prayerfully explore the effectiveness of ministry together can expect mutual growth. Mutually reviewing ministry can result in revitalizing mission and re-energizing pastors and people. Everyone wants to believe that what they are doing is worthwhile and makes a difference. Regular review gives the feedback necessary to continue moving forward in confidence that what everyone is striving for is a shared vision of the mission of the congregation in question.

CHAPTER II

Grounded in Theology

Americans have been strongly influenced by what we commonly call "The Protestant Work Ethic." Although we profess that we live by God's grace alone, most of us come dangerously close to slipping into a "works righteousness" mentality—if we work hard enough, do enough, are dedicated enough, God will bless our lives abundantly. This isn't a rational part of our thinking but a combination of deeply instilled beliefs about the value of hard work, our western definition of success, and our inability to believe that God loves us enough that we don't have to *do* anything to earn our salvation. This attitude affects both the "work" that earns us a living or provides a home for our family and the way we consider the success and effectiveness of others with whom we share life. Work is basically good. God chose not to work alone and so created human beings and placed them in the garden to preserve and nurture it (Genesis 2:15). We often forget this, focusing instead on Genesis 3:17-19 when God casts Adam and Eve from the garden and sentences them to a life of toil. Work was originally a blessing and a way in which human beings could be in partnership with God for the care of creation.

This work continues in whatever way we "earn our living" as managers and stewards of God's whole inhabited earth.[1] The Reformers valued work but embraced also the concept of "vocation"—the calling of each Christian to lead a faithful life. The way one lived out his or her Christian vocation was more important

than how one earned his or her keep. Liturgy means "the work of
the people." In other words, the priesthood of believers means that
all Christians are called to the work of ministry—not just those
called to Word and Sacrament.

"Evaluation is natural to the human experience. Evaluation is
one of God's ways of bringing the history of the past into dialogue
with the hope for the future. Without confession of sin there is no
reconciliation; without the counting of blessings there is no thanks-
giving; without the acknowledgment of accomplishments there is
no celebration; without awareness of potential there is no hope;
without hope there is no desire for growth; and without a desire for
growth the past will dwarf the future. We are called into new
growth and new ministries by taking a realistic and hopeful look at
what we have been and what we can still become. Surrounded by
God's grace and the crowd of witnesses in the faith, we can look at
our past unafraid and from its insights eagerly face the future with
new possibilities."[2] This wonderful quotation from a pamphlet
prepared by the Division of Ordained Ministry of the United
Methodist Church concisely presents a theological foundation for
ministry evaluation. Evaluation will happen—in parking lots, over
the telephone, in sincere and earnest conversations. To provide an
orderly and caring process by which evaluation can occur gives
integrity to the church's desire to be faithful to its call and mission.
Faith and covenant are the foundation for ministry evaluation.
Faith that trusts in the Holy Spirit to guide and direct our delibera-
tions, faith in the inherent goodness of each as well as the potential
for failure, faith that God's forgiveness is extended to us all when
we fall short of God's intent for our ministry. Covenant in that we
are bound to one another through Christ and called to partnership
in mission. All love requires accountability. God loves us but
calls us into account for the covenant we have made with God.
When the word *love* is changed to *accountable* in I John 4:20 we
find "We cannot be accountable to God whom we have not seen if
we are not willing to be accountable to our brother and sister,
whom we have seen."[3]

In evaluating our mutual ministry it is important that we keep in the forefront of our thinking the vision and behavior of the church in light of its story and the demands of the world. Faithfulness to the Gospel means regular scrutiny of what we say and do in applying the biblical mandate to contemporary life.[4] Roy Oswald in an On Demand Publication of The Alban Institute entitled *Getting a Fix on Your Ministry* turns to words developed by the early church to describe the church present in the world—Kerygma, Koinonia, and Diakonia.[5] These concepts of the Word proclaimed (Kerygma), the faithful in Christ-centered fellowship (Koinonia), and ministry to the world in need (Diakonia) are useful in expanding our biblical and theological discussion of evaluation. No matter how sophisticated a process or instrument may be, if it does not consider these three cornerstones it will be useless in assessing the ministry of a church or its professionals.

Last, we must consider briefly the importance of evaluation as a tool for Christian growth rather than a weapon against a perceived enemy. "We have this treasure in earthen vessels, to show that the transcendent power belongs to God and not to us" (2 Corinthians 4:7). Pastors, congregational leaders, and members are all earthen vessels. We can be excellent carriers, we can be full, we can be empty. But we need care in handling. Vessels can be turned over, chipped, and broken and the valuable resource inside lost.[6] Evaluations should further equip us to carry the Gospel into the world. They should never be used to punish. A theological understanding of justice demands that when evaluation reveals our inadequacies or failures, opportunity for change and growth should be available. This means that responsible congregations do not use an evaluation to "get rid of the pastor" and that ministers do not use an evaluation of a congregation as "reason to leave." We are in this together. Evaluation brings with it the possibility for renewal.

In Summary

Most individuals in the western world have a "work ethic" that
transfers into their expectations about competency in ministry.
Although God loves us regardless of what we do, we often assume
we can "earn" our salvation. Thus, work has always been an important aspect of our identity. It is easy for us to forget that the
work of the church does not rest on the clergy alone. When we
isolate the pastor for evaluation we risk slipping into the mindset
that the work of Christ in the world is only accomplished by those
called to ordained, professional ministry. Careful, reflective evaluation can result in Christian growth for both pastors and members
alike. We are called into accountability through our mutual commitment to Jesus Christ and his church. Evaluation should never
be used as a tool to tear down the Body of Christ but as one that
strengthens and builds up all who serve it.

CHAPTER III

Pitfalls and Potholes

It seems a bit odd to address the pitfalls of ministry evaluation before we even begin—but better safe than sorry! There are numerous ways in which evaluations can be sabatoged, some even before they are begun. Familiarity with them can save valuable time and energy and better assure a successful review.

The Chicken or the Egg?

Believe it or not—and I bet you believe it!—procrastination is one of the greatest enemies of evaluation. Procrastination can often take the form of a lengthy discussion of whether we can actually have a helpful evaluation when we have no ministry goals. Chief decision makers can put off a needed review while they debate and plan for goal setting, long-range planning, and other articulated objectives. As essential as planning is to the vitality of congregational life, to put off review in favor of a planning process (which will then be evaluated several years down the road) may open the congregation to serious problems. But how can you evaluate when there are no mission goals in place? It is more difficult but it certainly isn't impossible. The evaluation process can be used as a planning tool. This will be described in more detail in later chapters. All congregations can identify basic areas of ministry: worship, outreach, spiritual development, etc. Just asking the simplest question—"How are we doing here?"—can generate information that becomes the grist for future planning. Douglas Walrath suggests that congregations should be about two kinds of planning—basic planning (long-range for five years or more) and annual planning (which is done yearly and can be combined with annual review).[1] Lyle Schaller in his book *Create Your Own Future* provides numerous alternatives to the long-range planning process. He suggests that there are countless points of entry into planning—not just one![2] Whatever the resources you use to help you in planning and evaluation, don't allow yourselves to become immobilized because one or the other is not in place. Evaluation and planning are two sides to the same coin. It matters less *where* you start than that you start at all.

Tools Not Weapons!

Even though we recommend that evaluation occur in the context of reviewing the whole ministry of the congregation, we recognize that many times only the pastor is reviewed. All too often this evaluation is used as a weapon against the pastor. Judicatories are filled with horror stories of how an unauthorized "survey" on the pastor's effectiveness led to his or her termination. Awareness of the limitations and possible minefields in any evaluation process may help us to consider carefully when and how to engage in such reflection.

"Evaluation that is seen as judgment for the purposes of reward and punishment will be doomed to failure in the church."[3] One of the greatest pitfalls for evaluations is tying the process to compensation issues. This puts the pastor being evaluated into a position of needing to "prove his/her worth," putting a best foot forward, or not revealing areas that need attention. The fear of losing salary or not receiving even a cost of living raise may interfere with the minister's honest examination of his or her effectiveness, create a defensive atmosphere, or, at worst, encourage the camouflaging or even misrepresentation of important congregational issues. It is the experience of many that when financial reward is coupled with evaluation, the review cannot be an opportunity for growth. Therefore, the way to avoid this pitfall is to keep these two important processes completely separate. Fair and just pay for work rendered is a theological and moral issue for the church. Withholding salary increases, reducing compensation for unsatisfactory work, or even dangling the promise of greater dollars for "superior" performance are all inappropriate in the church. If performance isn't satisfactory, it should be dealt with straightforwardly—not punished by jeopardizing the financial security of the pastor and his/her family.

Ouch! Will the Truth Hurt?

In an interview, Roy Oswald, senior consultant for The Alban Institute, indicated that the longer a pastorate the more difficult it is to obtain quality feedback. Because most long-tenured pastors are open, warm, and accessible, they are usually deeply loved. No one wants to "hurt" the pastor, and so often people withhold constructive information that, in fact, could be valuable for the minister's growth. Unfortunately, these "feeling" types also have greater difficulty accepting criticism—even that given in good faith. It takes only one episode when the pastor's feelings were hurt to curb a congregation's willingness to share concerns.

The best way to avoid this pitfall is never to evaluate the pastor without evaluating the entire ministry of the church (are you getting the point by now?). The pastor who truly wants the feedback must say clearly and *repeatedly* that he or she needs this information in order to stay fresh and effective in ministry. Providing a supportive environment for learning parishioners' perceptions of the strengths and growing edges of one's ministry can also keep these lines of communication open. Finally, assuring the congregation that whatever information comes through the review will *not* be used for salary determination or to decide the future of the pastoral relationship can ease this concern.[4]

Tasks Vs. Roles

It is generally accepted that ninety percent of what clergy do is invisible to ninety percent of the laity ninety percent of the time! When we mention the word "pastor," what comes to mind is formed by what each of us has come to expect from that role. Reducing ministry to just a series of tasks ignores what is much more significant: the many *roles* of the pastor. The minister does not practice religion as a lawyer does law or a doctor medicine. The doctor or the lawyer rarely try to change the client's life goals. The minister has a far more complicated relationship with parishioners, making success or failure far harder to measure.[5] Diane Fassel, co-author of the *Addictive Organization*, points out that "the church is the only organization in creation whose ultimate goals are the salvation of humankind, the elimination of world hunger, and the liberation of the politically and economically oppressed."[6] Much evaluation of ministry is based on totally subjective reflection. Who really decides if that sermon was a ten or a two? The person who is bitter about his inability to save his marriage despite pastoral counseling will evaluate "pastoral care" differently, perhaps, than the couple with whom the pastor spent four long nights in the hospital while an infant struggled for life. Most of what pastors do just can't be measured that easily! Functional performance can be more accurately assessed than role dimension.[7] Avoiding the confusing pitfall of subjectivity is impossible. Being aware of it, however, and using a variety of evaluation techniques with as wide a congregational sampling as possible will more likely reveal relevant patterns. Doing just the opposite—consulting only individuals with whom the pastor has had a direct relationship in one area of ministry to evaluate *only* that area—may also be helpful. The model used at St. Mark's Episcopal Church in Chapter Four provides further reflection on subjectivity in review.

Finally, be aware that no one evaluation technique can do it all. There are drawbacks and shortcomings to every process. While a questionnaire with numerical ratings can reach a large number of people quickly, it may produce only shallow information. Interviews may probe the depths of an area of ministry, but they are time consuming, reach fewer people, and yield information that may be difficult to correlate. An outside consultant brings expertise but may also bring biases. Being aware of the limitations of whatever procedures are used and, when possible, tailoring the process to the unique needs of a particular ministry can balance the assets of such techniques with the liabilities.

In Summary

Procrastination never serves us! Now is as good a time as any to get started. Anytime we begin to focus on human situations we find ourselves in an area of subjective opinions. Some things can be easily measured: Did she or did she not teach four adult Bible studies during Advent? Other aspects are not so clearly assessed: Was she a good teacher? Did the congregation grow in the understanding of the Scriptures? Evaluations that are tied to compensation prohibit healthy assessment. All processes have strengths and limitations. People don't like to criticize loved pastors and are quick to decimate unloved ones! Evaluations are most helpful during times when things are going well, not when conflict looms large. Evaluating the pastor's ministry along with that of the congregation minimizes the anxiety an evaluation creates. Staying aware of these potential pitfalls and determining how we will acknowledge them (or avoid them when possible) can improve the possibilities for a useful evaluation.

CHAPTER IV

We Did It!

Nothing convinces like a success story—people who have taken on the tasks with which we struggle and made them work. In this chapter we will consider four such congregations and pastors, each unique in the approach to evaluation.

Ashby First Parish Church, Unitarian Universalist

A Small Parish Reflects in a Big Way

Catherine Holmes Clark, a free-lance writer, had served on every committee in her thirty-member Unitarian church when a malaise began to creep across the congregation. Low key grumbling and rumblings, sometimes directed toward their part-time pastor, began to take a toll on the morale of this strong parish in a small country town in Massachusetts. Catherine, an astute observer of human dynamics, was convinced that the problem lay not entirely with the pastor but with the entire parish's ministry. Once again she volunteered to moderate a committee, this time to review the effectiveness of Ashby First Parish Church's mission. Catherine went to the heart of ministry and began asking the questions, What is the purpose of the Church? Of *our* church? Have our activities become simply dead rituals or habits? How do we revitalize our commitment to a vision? After a frustrating search through questionnaires used by other Unitarian churches, Catherine designed and copyrighted an evaluation process that allows the pastor, each committee, and the congregational membership to scrutinize the ministry of one another leading to a deeper covenant of ministry as a shared experience. That was almost ten years ago. Today, Ashby First Parish Church is about to undertake the process again, this time as part of a "temperature taking" following the completion of two years in a new pastoral relationship. Catherine has granted permission to share a summary of her model that is adaptable in many ways to fit a variety of congregational sizes and needs. Her entire model is available as an On Demand Publication of The Alban Institute.[1]

The Process

The "Annual Church Review Procedure" recommends that a committee be formed to conduct and report on the evaluation process. There should be an overall Review Coordinator, a member willing to oversee the review of the congregation, one for the review of the committees, and one for the review of the pastor. The Review Coordinator works with the summary of each review section and prepares the final report.

Every member of the congregation receives the whole-church evaluation in the mail and is requested to return it or give it to a canvasser who visits them. In addition they receive an optional questionnaire evaluating the minister that they are urged also to complete. The congregation's form covers four areas: acknowledging accomplishments, rating congregational performance, identifying strengths and weaknesses, and planning. Members are asked to look back on goals established at the last annual meeting of the parish and to rate them as accomplished, partly accomplished, or not accomplished. They are also asked to comment on goals not accomplished and on those they identify as particularly significant. Using a scale of one (exceptional) to five (needs a lot of work!) members are asked to rate the effectiveness of the congregation in sixteen areas ranging from "Fulfilling Our Purpose" (example: ___We have a community, a family of people who can depend on each other and take responsibility for each other) to "Budgeting Time and Energy" (example: ___The church uses its human resources wisely, prioritizing projects and distributing responsibility widely). At the end of the form an invitation is extended to list those areas of strength worthy of special note, those areas needing improvement, and suggestions for future projects or programs. When the whole-church forms are collected and tabulated, the summary is submitted to the Parish Committee and published in the newsletter prior to the Annual Meeting.

At the same time members are reviewing their ministry, the committees of the church are using their current job description, their report to the last annual meeting containing goals for the current year being reviewed, and a review form to reflect on their effectiveness. They are examining both their own work as a group and that of the minister. The minister also gives feedback to them on how he or she views the work of the committee. When the process is complete, the committee determines what information will remain confidential and then prepares a report for the Annual Meeting. This report includes a list of accomplishments, goals for the coming year, and any changes recommended in the job description for that committee. The questionnaire and process for committee review is similar to that of the congregation. After being asked to reflect on accomplishments, members are asked to evaluate a variety of tasks listed under the headings of *Effective Lay Leadership, Administrative Skills, Budgeting Time and Energy, Outreach, General Work and Communication Skills, Attitudes,* and *Getting Our Specific Job Done.* After considering strengths and areas needing further attention, committee members turn their comments to planning for the next year and are invited to suggest options and volunteer for particular service.

The final aspect of a mutual ministry review involves feedback to the pastor. In Catherine Clark's model this is done by a Ministry Committee. They use the returned questionnaires from members of the congregation, a longer form completed by the minister

and each member of the Ministry Committee, and informal interviews with a cross section of the congregation. The pastor and the
committee examine the compiled data, discuss the implications for
the pastor's continuing education, determine what will remain confidential, and then prepare a report that goes to the Annual Meeting
along with the pastor's contract. The shorter form, which goes to
each member of the congregation, includes a list of descriptive
statements such as "___ sermons inspire, clarify, and stimulate" and
"___ pursues a program to attract, welcome, and involve new members." The longer form for Ministry Committee members divides
the pastor's performance into several major areas for a similar
numerical evaluation. An important part of the summary of the
minister's review includes his or her identifying and agreeing on
long-term career and personal goals.

The *Annual Church Review Procedure* includes a time line
chart for each of the three aspects of review and suggestions for
how the process may be adapted. It provides a useful and balanced
guide to evaluation as a *shared* experience reminding us once
again that the responsibility for effective ministry belongs to all the
people and not just to the pastor!

The McKinley Church and Foundation

Co-Pastors/Campus Ministers Request a Comprehensive Review

In the middle of some of the richest agricultural land in the nation
rests the community of Champaign/Urbana Illinois, best known
for the University of Illinois and the fighting Illini basketball team.
The McKinley Church and Foundation, a Presbyterian congregation and campus ministry, has been responding to the needs of
students and the community since 1906 as the first Land Grant
University congregation to establish a church just for students.
The congregation of 180 members welcomes 350 students as

active participants in worship and programs. An additional forty
students live in Presby House, a brick home adjacent to the church.
The McKinley Foundation is the campus ministry outreach of the
congregation and is governed by an elected board composed of
congregational members, community leaders, pastors, and representatives from other churches in the area. Over 2,500 students,
faculty and visitors pass through the doors of the McKinley Church
and Foundation *each week* to participate in the many programs, to
see an undergraduate art show, attend a gay/lesbian coffee house,
find a quiet place to study, worship at the Black Pentecostal church
that also uses the facility or, perhaps, to sleep at the shelter for
homeless men in the basement of the sanctuary.

The complexity of ministry in this exciting yet hectic setting
led co-pastors Steven Shoemaker and Charles Sweitzer to request a
comprehensive review of their effectiveness when Steve approached
his fifth year of service. Charlie has served McKinley since 1973
as an associate pastor. Steve arrived as head of staff in 1981. In
1983 at their request, the session recommended they become co-
pastors and the congregation agreed! In 1986, it seemed like a
good idea to ask, "How are we doing?"

Dr. Wynette Barnard, a member of the McKinley Church and
Foundation, was asked for help with the process. She wss a faculty
member of the College of Education at the University of Illinois
and now serves as Manager of National Programs for Resource
Careers, a Cleveland, Ohio firm assisting dual career couples in
relocation. Dr. Barnard designed the process that was used in 1986
and again in 1991. The process was led by the Personnel, Goals,
and Objectives Committee, which was composed of members of
both the Session (congregational decision makers) and the Board
(campus ministry decision makers). Every member and participating adult as well as additional individuals in the greater Champaign/
Urbana community was invited to respond to a questionnaire for
each of the two pastors. The Session and the Foundation Board
responded to an additional set of questions as did representatives
from the denominational judicatories of the Presbyterian Church

(USA). An interview guideline was prepared for use with a sampling of individuals from each of the above categories. The entire review process took three months to complete. At the conclusion of the process the Personnel, Goals, and Objectives Committee met individually with the pastors to discuss the results. The resulting report was then shared with the Session and Foundation Board.

In an interview with Steve and Charlie, I asked what growth had occurred between the 1986 and 1991 evaluations. Both indicated they were able to measure significant changes in their pastoral effectiveness based on changes made following the first evaluation. In 1986 Steve had received feedback that, in the face of his attempt to allow the elected leadership to truly "lead," the Session/ Board sometimes didn't know what *he* thought about particular issues. This came out in comments such as "Provide more leadership," and "We don't know what you think!" Steve realized that sharing his own opinion was not only appropriate at times, but helpful to his partners in ministry. The 1991 evaluation made much less mention of this earlier perception. Steve further indicated that, although his sermons generally received very high marks, some members believed his delivery needed work. He experimented with preaching from an outline rather than a manuscript and intentionally working to establish more eye contact with the congregation, with the result that there was very little mention of sermon delivery as an issue in the 1991 evaluation. For his part, Charlie had received feedback that people were bothered by his smoking in meetings, something he had not realized. Not only did Charlie refrain from smoking in the church, he quit altogether! Following the 1986 evaluation, Charlie also made a list of personal goals which included strategies for better self care and re-examining his commitments outside the McKinley community. In 1991 he reports feeling much better about the amount of judicatory service, nonmember weddings, and other tasks he performs in addition to his McKinley priorities.

Both pastors report that feedback on how their relationship to one another is perceived by others has been invaluable in strengthening the co-pastorate. Intentional work in the area of communication and seeking the assistance of an outside consultant to work on the perceived "gentle stress" in their relationship are examples of how they are currently using the learnings of the evaluation.

While both Charlie and Steve feel good about the results of the review process, they indicated ways they hope it can become stronger. Sharing summaries of the review with the congregation through the newsletter may help both pastors to talk more freely with others about the outcome. Establishing a support committee to work with them toward the goals resulting from the evaluation is another idea being considered. When introduced to the possibility of "mutual ministry" review of the congregation/session/board the interest of both of these creative pastors was piqued. Steve suggested that the influence of feminist thinking in the church may help congregations be much more open to holistic review. The potential to evaluate the effectiveness of the *entire* ministry of the congregation and not just the pastors furthers this way of thinking. I for one will eagerly await the 1996 review of this exciting ministry!

AN EVALUATION PROCESS
FOR THE MCKINLEY CHURCH/FOUNDATION[2]
Dr. Wynette Barnard, Designer
Spring, 1986

Introduction

It is the responsibility of the Personnel, Goals, and Objectives committee of the McKinley Presbyterian Church and Foundation to evaluate the co-pastors' work performance on an annual basis. This process generally involves a self-evaluation by each pastor with an external review by committee members. The evaluation is conducted each Fall, and results are *utilized* for personal improvement and in salary determination. During the Fall of 1985, the co-pastors suggested that a more comprehensive evaluation, considering input from both internal and external sources, would be valuable for their personal development. Thus a comprehensive evaluation was planned for spring, 1986. The purpose of this evaluation was to provide feedback to the pastors from the many people and organizations with whom they work, including people from within McKinley—the congregation, session members, board of directors and staff—as well as people within the Champaign/ Urbana community and the Presbyterian Church at the district, state and/or national level.

Method of Evaluation

The method of evaluation includes telephone interviews of representatives of community and church organizations and written questionnaires distributed to the congregation, session members, board of directors, and staff.

Sample
The sample includes all members of the congregation in attendance at either of two Sunday morning worship services, all members of the session and board of directors, and all staff and representatives of the larger church and community organizations. The number of respondents is reported in each section of the report.

Instruments
Written questionnaires and interview guides are provided based on the key questions identified for each audience. Copies of the instruments follow this description.

Procedure
Telephone interviews are to be conducted with representatives of church and community organizations during March and April, 1986. Written questionnaires are distributed to the congregation, session, board of directors, and staff.

Purpose and Focus of the Evaluation

The purpose of this evaluation is to assess the work performance of the co-pastors of McKinley Presbyterian Church and Foundation. In order to gain input from a variety of sources, six audiences have been identified: McKinley congregation, session, board of directors, staff, surrounding community, and larger Church.

To guide the evaluation process, six broad questions were identified. These questions are:

1. How does the McKinley congregation view the quality of the co-pastors' work?

2. How do McKinley session members view the quality and quantity of the co-pastors' work in areas related to the session's responsibility?

3. How do members of the McKinley Foundation Board of Directors view the quality and quantity of the co-pastors' work in areas related to the board's responsibility?

4. How does the McKinley staff view the quality of the co-pastors' management and supervision?

5. What is the quantity and quality of the co-pastors' participation in the larger Church?

6. What is the quantity and quality of the co-pastors' participation in community organizations?

Specific key questions were then identified for each audience to guide the collection of information. These follow on the attached questionnaires.

SUGGESTIONS FOR TELEPHONE INTERVIEWING

I've developed a script as a means to share some of the key points that should be made in the interview. This is just a guideline, so please improve upon it in any way and/or adapt it to the person/agency with which you are talking.

Hello, I'm _____ from McKinley Presbyterian Church and Foundation. Our pastor, Charlie Sweitzer/Steve Shoemaker, has requested a committee to conduct a comprehensive evaluation of his performance, including his involvement in organizations outside of McKinley.

Steve/Charlie has provided us with your name as a person who would know something about and might be willing to share information about his involvement with _____ *(their organization).* All of the interview information will be kept confidential and reported only in a group summary.

Would you be willing to answer a few questions about Steve/Charlie's activities within _____ *(their organization)*?

(If they say NO) —
That's fine, thank you for your time.
(Don't push, some people prefer not to be involved in evaluations.)

(If they say YES) —
Would you have about five or ten minutes now or would you prefer that I call at a different time?

(Set up time or continue.)

Questions *(next page)*

Thank you for time and feedback.

*Overall, we should leave people with the impression that they are doing **us** a favor, that we don't want to inconvenience them, and that we sincerely appreciate their time.*

TELEPHONE INTERVIEW QUESTIONS

Person being evaluated:　　　□ Steve　　□ Charlie

Interviewee is a member of _____.

1. In what ways has Steve/Charlie participated in this organization/committee?

2. What has been your connection with Steve/Charlie?

3. How has his participation benefited this organization/committee?

4. In your opinion, what are his strengths related to his participation in this organization/committee?

5. In what ways might he improve his performance to further benefit this organization/committee?

6. If you were to rate his overall effectiveness on a scale of 1 (low) to 5 (high), where would you rate him?

　　　　1　　2　　3　　4　　5

MEMBER/PARTICIPANT
EVALUATION FORM FOR CO-PASTORS

This form is for feedback on _____.

Directions: Please read each statement and indicate the extent to which you agree or disagree by circling the appropriate letters:

SD = Strongly Disagree
D = Disagree
U = Undecided
A = Agree
SA = Strongly Agree
NA = Not Applicable

Morning Worship—**When he leads morning worship, I feel that he:**

1. nurtures my spiritual needs.　　SD　　D　　U　　SA　　NA

2. challenges me to implement　　SD　　D　　U　　SA　　NA
   the Christian message in my .
   life.

3. enhances my understanding　　SD　　D　　U　　SA　　NA
   of the Christian faith.

4. selects appropriate/interesting　　SD　　D　　U　　SA　　NA
   topics for the sermon.

5. provides variety in the focus　　SD　　D　　U　　SA　　NA
   of sermons.

   (If you disagree, indicate if there is too much (+) or too little (-) emphasis on: ___issues, ___people concerns, ___Bible, ___other _____.)

6. effectively conducts the prayers　SD　　D　　U　　SA　　NA
   of the people.

7. chooses appropriate hymns.　　SD　　D　　U　　SA　　NA

8. effectively leads communion.　　SD　　D　　U　　SA　　NA

Personal contact/Counseling—In my personal contact and/or in counseling, I feel that he:

9. is easy to talk with.   SD   D   U   SA   NA

10. understands my individual   SD   D   U   SA   NA
    concerns.

11. knows what he's doing in   SD   D   U   SA   NA
    trying to help me.

12. has a sensitive understanding SD   D   U   SA   NA
    of my most obvious feelings.

13. has helped me to explore my   SD   D   U   SA   NA
    concerns.

14. made a helpful referral when   SD   D   U   SA   NA
    appropriate.

15. is someone I would talk with   SD   D   U   SA   NA
    again.

Teaching—When I attend classes/workshops taught by him, I feel that he:

16. is organized and prepared.   SD   D   U   SA   NA

17. is knowledgeable about the   SD   D   U   SA   NA
    subject matter.

18. is interested/enthusiastic   SD   D   U   SA   NA
    about the subject matter.

19. is responsive to the needs   SD   D   U   SA   NA
    of participants.

20. utilizes a teaching style appro- SD   D   U   SA   NA
    priate for the subject matter
    and participants.

21. is an effective teacher.   SD   D   U   SA   NA

Working with small groups—When I have worked with him in small groups within the church, I have found that he:

22. regularly attends meetings.   SD   D   U   SA   NA

23. actively participates in dis-   SD   D   U   SA   NA
cussion and activities.

24. provides leadership when   SD   D   U   SA   NA
appropriate.

25. is open to other points of   SD   D   U   SA   NA
view or suggestions.

26. fulfills his responsibilities.   SD   D   U   SA   NA

27. is effective in working with   SD   D   U   SA   NA
small groups.

Ministry beyond the congregation—From what I have observed, heard about, or been involved with, I feel that he:

28. is actively involved in ministry   SD   D   U   SA   NA
beyond the congregation.

29. has selected appropriate   SD   D   U   SA   NA
groups, issues, or benefits
with which to work.

30. spends an appropriate amount   SD   D   U   SA   NA
of time in outside activities.

     (If you disagree, indicate [x] ___too much time, ___too little time.)

31. is effective in his ministry be-   SD   D   U   SA   NA
yond the congregation.

32. helps establish a positive   SD   D   U   SA   NA
image of the McKinley com-
munity.

33. In your opinion, what are his strengths?

34. In what ways might he change to improve his performance?

35. Other comments.

SAMPLE LETTER

(Single person households are receiving duplicates for each staff member because of bulk mailing specifications that all pieces in a mailing need to be identical.)

To the McKinley Community:

Steve Shoemaker and Charlie Sweitzer have requested that the Personnel Committee conduct a comprehensive evaluation of their performance. As a part of this evaluation, we would like *your* input concerning the quality of the co-pastor's performance. Your responses will be treated confidentially and reported only in a group summary. Honest feedback is greatly appreciated!

Please fill out a separate form for each person (forms are labeled). The completed forms may be placed in the box at the back of the Church or in the Foundation, sent to the Foundation, or sent to Russell Zwoyer, 2008B Eagle Ridge Court, Urbana, Illinois 61801.

Thank you for participating in this evaluation.

Personnel Committee

This form is to be used for the performance evaluation of

Charlie

SESSION MEMBER/FOUNDATION BOARD
EVALUATION FORM FOR CO-PASTORS

This form is for feedback on _____.

Directions: Please read each statement and indicate the extent to which you agree or disagree by circling the appropriate letters:

> SD = Strongly Disagree
> D = Disagree
> U = Undecided
> A = Agree
> SA = Strongly Agree
> NA = Not Applicable

As a result of participating on the board of directors, I feel that he:

1. keeps the members of the board informed of his activities.   SD   D   U   SA   NA

2. is open to suggestions and/or input concerning his responsibilities.   SD   D   U   SA   NA

3. follows through on suggestions.   SD   D   U   SA   NA

4. fulfills his responsibilities.   SD   D   U   SA   NA

5. participates in appropriate committees.   SD   D   U   SA   NA

If you participate in a subcommittee, please respond to questions 6-10 (if not, skip to #11).

As a result of participating on _____ committee, I feel that he:

6. regularly attends meetings.   SD   D   U   SA   NA

7. actively participates in the meetings.   SD   D   U   SA   NA

8. provides leadership when   SD   D   U   SA   NA
    appropriate.

9. fulfills responsibility within the SD   D   U   SA   NA
    committee.

10. effectively communicates   SD   D   U   SA   NA
    information, ideas, concerns.

Overall, I feel that he:

11. is leading the church and   SD   D   U   SA   NA
    foundation in a positive
    direction.

12. allocates his time appropriately. SD   D   U   SA   NA

13. is effective in his ministry role. SD   D   U   SA   NA

14. In your opinion, what are his strengths?

15. In what ways might he change to improve his performance?

16. Other comments (use back).

STAFF EVALUATION FORM FOR CO-PASTORS

This form is for feedback on _____.

Directions: Please read each statement and indicate the extent to which you agree or disagree by circling the appropriate letters:

> SD = Strongly Disagree
> D = Disagree
> U = Undecided
> A = Agree
> SA = Strongly Agree
> NA = Not Applicable

As my supervisor, I feel that he:

1. provides a clear understanding   SD   D   U   SA   NA
   of my responsibilities.

2. effectively communicates his   SD   D   U   SA   NA
   expectations concerning my
   performance.

3. makes reasonable demands.   SD   D   U   SA   NA

4. allows me to participate in the   SD   D   U   SA   NA
   decision-making process.

5. allows me to work   SD   D   U   SA   NA
   independently.

6. is available when I need help   SD   D   U   SA   NA
   or guidance in carrying out my
   responsibilities.

7. respects and supports my   SD   D   U   SA   NA
   abilities and role.

8. provides feedback on my   SD   D   U   SA   NA
   performance.

9. is sensitive to my personal   SD   D   U   SA   NA
    feelings.

10. is an effective supervisor.   SD   D   U   SA   NA

11. In your opinion what are his strengths as a supervisor?

12. In what ways might he change to improve his performance?

13. Other comments.

Bethlehem Evangelical Lutheran Church

A Mutual Ministry Review

Almost twelve years ago Pastor Antti Lepisto came to serve the people of Bethlehem Evangelical Lutheran Church in DeKalb, Illinois. From day one he began to implement his strong conviction that ministry is a mutual task with shared joys and responsibilities. This five-hundred-plus congregation still has lingering ties to the Finnish settlers who founded the congregation in this town of 33,000 sixty miles west of Chicago. A student of organizational development, Antti understood the necessity for regular reflection on his own ministry and that of the congregation and formed a Mutual Ministry Committee to do just that.

The Mutual Ministry Committee begins its work early in the year and concludes in September with an update on progress towards the goals established earlier. In evaluating Pastor Lepisto's ministry the committee turned to the work of Lyle Schaller using his list of fourteen activities of the pastor: administration, community leadership, continuing education, counseling, denominational and ecumenical responsibilities, evangelism, personal and family life, preaching, social ministry, stewardship, teaching, theology, bereavement and crisis visitation, and worship. The committee uses a common definition for each of these tasks so that all may understand the task the same way. Antti comes to the February meeting with a self-evaluation of each of these tasks in ministry and presents his suggested list of priorities for the upcoming year. The committee then meets without Antti to review his evaluation and develop their own list of priorities for his work. At a third meeting both Antti and the Mutual Ministry Committee reflect on the two priority lists, the evaluative comments of the committee on last year's work, and any negotiations regarding the adjustment of the priority list. The final priority list does not include all fourteen tasks, acknowledging that no pastor can do all with the same effectiveness. The following is an example of the lists:

Pastor Lepisto's Priorities	Committee's Comments
1) Preaching	You should delegate more worship leader ship and details regarding worship. It's okay if others fail occasionally!
2) Administration	
3) Worship	
4) Sick, Crisis, Bereavement Adminisration	Counseling—you don't need to do it all but we're concerned that people get the help they need—refer?
5) Personal/Family	Ride your bike while visiting!
6) Evangelism	Perhaps this should be a higher priority! Others may be trained to help. We want new members.
7) Stewardship	Why are you concerned? You can use the newsletter and key people.
8) Teaching	
9) Social Ministry	This should be done by the congregation— not a high priority for the pastor's time.
10) Theology	
11) Counseling	What do you mean? Put this lower. It's also related to preaching and worship.
12) Denominational/Ecumenical	Perhaps this needs to be higher or tied into administration and teaching. Support groups and booklet rsources!
13) Continuing Education	It may be low, but we know you rank it higher!
14) Community Involvement	Again, it may be low, but WE KNOW BETTER!

The Mutual Ministry Committee's comment on the Pastor's Prepared Evaluation—"Good thought into this review! A- for the
year!" The Mutual Ministry Committee's priority list for the same
pastoral priorities was as follows:

1) Preaching/Worship (same as pastor's)
2) Administration (same as pastor's)
3) Evangelism (pastor ranked 6)
4) All Counseling—sick, bereavement, crisis, pastoral (visitation same as pastor, pastoral counseling ranked 11)
5) Teaching (pastor ranked 8)
6) Continuing Education (pastor ranked 13)
7) Denominational and Ecumenical Relationship (pastor
   ranked 12)
8) Administration of Social Ministry (pastor ranked social
   ministry 9)
9) Community Involvement

The Mutual Ministry Committee chose to identify only nine
priorities for the coming year even though Pastor Lepisto had
ranked all fourteen.

In reflecting on the above, it is important to note how the
Mutual Ministry Committee edited the skills as in "administration
of social ministry" rather than "social ministry," further clarifying
how they viewed the pastor's appropriate involvement in this important aspect of mission. The observation of the committee that
the pastor actually valued continuing education and denomina-
tional/ecumenical involvement higher than he listed them *and* the
committee's agreement that these were, in fact, important priorities
by their higher ranking is also interesting to note. When the committee and the pastor met together to share reflections and negoti-
ate the priorities, Pastor Lepisto was convinced that the committee's
list should become his for the coming year. He assured me, however, that in other years priorities were often established after conversation that reflected some of both lists and even added a few!

After this meeting the Mutual Ministry Committee sends a report to the Church Council, who can further edit or change the report before it is communicated to the congregation. In September the Committee meets again with the pastor to review the progress toward the priorities and goals established earlier. In an interview with Pastor Lepisto, he said, "As an INFP (Myers-Briggs Personality Type), I have found that the review process has helped me prioritize my time and energy together with the help of a good group of folks. It has given me something to measure against. They have helped me set boundaries and set achievable goals which are future oriented."

An important additional piece of this process is a June meeting with the pastor's spouse and family. This meeting is held without the pastor present and is intended to show pastoral care for the family of the minister. Discussion ranges from managing the stress of being a clergy family to needs in the manse. This sensitive, thoughtful approach to the inclusion of the entire family in the review process is an important part of Bethlehem Evangelical Lutheran Church's attitude toward ministry.

Last, but equally important to our discussion of mutual ministry, is the review of the congregation's ministry. In 1989 the Council and Pastor Lepisto determined that *all* the ministry of the congregation should be evaluated, not just the pastor's. They sought the consulting services of The Rev. Gary Wollersheim in St. Charles, Illinois, to lead them in a process. An Ad Hoc Review Team was established to work with Gary, and a thorough study and review of the life of the congregation was conducted. This study identified the strengths of Bethlehem Lutheran's ministry and also areas that needed to be addressed. Recommendations that resulted from the review included such insights as the need for two worship services and a more focused outreach to students at the nearby Northern Illinois University. The Council and the Pastor of this healthy Lutheran parish agree that this added dimension of congregational evaluation is essential to future growth and fulfillment of their mission. They intend to add periodic reflection by a consultant and ad hoc committee to future reviews.

St. Mark's Episcopal Church

Maintaining Vitality in the Long Pastorate

There are times when it is appropriate to focus a review just on the pastor's effectiveness. Obviously, ministers who are able to engage in creative and effective ministry in one setting for over a period of ten years or more are not only capable but often willing to reflect on their own strengths and growing edges. One such pastor is the Rev. James R. Adams, rector for twenty-five years of St. Mark's Episcopal Church on Capitol Hill in Washington, D.C. St. Mark's is a parish with 640 adult members, a staff of two full-time clergy, and a large programmatic staff to cover the many artistic and mission efforts. One half of the membership live within walking distance of the church and are mainly young, white professionals.

Jim Adams indicated that earlier in his ministry "evaluation" meant only hearing the "negative" comments. He would be at best disgruntled and at worst would focus on his failings, unable to balance them with the positive feedback coming his way. Jim decided that if he was to maintain his vital yet demanding ministry at St. Mark's he needed a balanced, fair way to assess his effectiveness that allowed for both the celebration of successes and identification of areas in which to grow. At Jim's request and with the assistance of Priscilla Adams (no relation), a member of St. Mark's, and Dr. Clinton Kelly, a consultant and Presbyterian layman, a process was developed to conduct just such a review. It was formally published as "Evaluation of the Clergy—Here's How," an On Demand Publication of The Alban Institute, and permission has been granted to include the entire model as part of this resource. The process as used by Jim Adams at St. Mark's includes the formation of a review committee (eight to ten members) that gives a *significant* amount of time to this task for one year. Because of the nature of this thorough process, it is recommended that it occur once every four years. You will note that there is a subjective

element to the evaluation process. Jim stated that in his experience
the committee becomes highly skilled in sorting through subjective
responses. Using the definition of counseling as "when others seek
Jim out" and ministry as " when Jim seeks out others", the committee becomes clear that sometimes when Jim's best work is done
people still may not be satisfied. This mature way of examining
the elusive aspects of ministry can provide invaluable feedback to
a pastor. What follows next is the process Jim has found so helpful
in evaluating his ongoing ministry at St. Mark's.

EVALUATION OF THE CLERGY: HERE'S HOW
by James R. Adams and Priscilla Adams

Preface

"You are out of your mind, or smoking pot, if you think we can
evaluate Jim much less agree to a numerical grade on his performance! Besides, that is the Vestry's job not ours!" Eighteen
months later the Clergy Development Committee happily reported
to the Vestry that they had indeed evaluated the parish priest and
even given him a numerical grade. Most important, there was
absolute consensus on the numerical grades, and the reasons for
the grades, on each of the ten separate major categories (such as
leadership, worship, Christian Education, etc.) and on the weighted
value (importance) of each category.

We felt good! Jim felt good! The Vestry was pleased! We
had something solid to build on—to use to improve our church, our
minister, ourselves, and we were sure that it would please God.

We used a method known as Decision Analysis that has grown
out of some original work in a probability theory by a Catholic
priest in the 1800's and some utility theory that has more recently
emerged. Clinton Kelly, Ph. D. taught us how to apply the principles of Decision Analysis. Dr. Kelly, a Presbyterian and a
learned man, guided us through the initial stages, kept us focused,

and critiqued our work. In the process we came to understand and appreciate the principles he had put before us:

First, the Vestry (or official lay governing board) simply does not have the time—nor the detachment—to conduct an evaluation;

Second, the evaluation must be comprehensive but all of the functions, or facets, must be aggregated into a workable number of ten to twelve categories;

Third, everyone must agree on what constitutes good and what constitutes poor performance in each of the major categories;

Fourth, a numerical score—no matter how difficult or onerous—*must* be assigned;

Fifth, some confidentiality is essential; and, finally,

Sixth, the report must be used as a springboard for corrective action and positive growth.

Evaluation is a difficult job and it takes a lot of time. In our opinion it need not be done every year. Every third or fourth year is adequate. It takes dedication, patience, and understanding, but it is an extremely worthwhile learning and growth enhancing experience. We recommend that you try it. Without doubt we can say, "You'll like it."

Randall H. Prothro
Clergy Development Committee

The Process

Step One—Appoint the Committee

The pastor and governing board, having agreed to embark on a process of evaluation for the pastor, authorize the senior lay official to appoint a committee representing a cross section of the congregation. In consultation with the pastor, the senior lay official considers age, marital status, sex, and philosophy in making the appointments so that most of the points of view within the congregation will have representation. The pastor and the governing board agree to the selection of one of the members to chair the committee.

The committee members must understand that the success of the venture depends on singleness of purpose—evaluating the pastor's work in the congregation. For genuine evalution to emerge from people with a wide diversity of viewpoints, they will have to work for a true consensus and not be satisfied with superficial agreement.

In approaching the task, people will need to remember that they can usefully identify their expectations and reactions to the pastor's functioning in the role of ordained minister, but they cannot be of much help if they become fixed on questions of personality. Pastors can learn new skills and improve their performance in many areas, but they cannot do much about changing their basic personalities.

Step Two—Establish Categories

Two members of the committee should be assigned to list all of the areas in which the pastor is expected to function in the congregation, such as worship or counseling. This list can then be reduced by the whole committee to ten or twelve categories.

This will involve some combining or aggregation of areas and even the elimination of the least important ones. The resulting list will be the categories used for evaluation.

Step Three—Rank the Categories

This is perhaps the most difficult task of all, but keep moving and don't worry because you can make changes up to the very end. First, just place the most important category at the top of a page and the least important at the bottom; then roughly place all the rest in between at about the level you think their importance warrants.

We put Leadership at the top and Community Activities at the bottom. Then we put Worship close to but below Leadership and then put three very close together—Christian Education, Ministering, and Counseling. We switched those three around before we finally settled on the right order for our church.

Now you must assign a numerical weight to each category. We gave Leadership a 100. Worship we decided was nearly equal to Leadership so we gave it a 90. We were balancing items that appeared to be of equal weight. We had to look at the whole list and compare each category with all of the others to decide which functions were really the most important to us. Then we looked at Christian Education, Ministering, and Counseling and decided they were about the same in importance and that all three together were equal to Worship which we had weighted at 90. So we assigned 31 to Christian Education, which we thought was a tiny bit more important than Ministering, to which we gave a 30 and Counseling to which we assigned a 29.

The final task in this step is a purely mathematical one of converting the assigned weights which are from 0 to 100 to a percentage by normalizing them to 100. Just add all weights—100, 90, 31, 30, 29, etc.—then divide each of the weights by the total, multiply by 100, and you have the normalized weight. In this case, Leadership became 31%, Worship 28%, and the next three 9%, in round numbers.

Step Four—Allocate Time

Each of the normalized weights now becomes the percent of available time that will be spent on each category. For instance, you will spend 30% of your time in each succeeding step working on Worship, 11% on Christian Education, etc. This discipline will help you to avoid spending too much time on the unimportant categories which, of course, are the easiest and least anxiety producing matters.

Step Five—Determine the Criteria

The evaluation committee and the pastor are now ready to prepare the criteria to be used in the evaluation of the pastor's work in each category.

The most direct way to establish the criteria is to ask yourselves as you consider a specific area of the pastor's responsibility, "What would the best possible performance look like?" "What would the worst possible performance look like?" For example, under the category Worship, you might want to include your expectations about preaching. Your criteria under that category should state clearly what you mean when you say, "That was an outstanding sermon," or "That was an awful sermon."

You will need between five and ten criteria for evaluation in each category. The form to be used in reporting on each category should look like this. This is only an example. You will work out your own categories, criteria, and scoring.

Category: Worship

The best possible performance in worship will include:

1. Preaching sermons that relate God's word to our lives.

2. Providing leadership and instruction in the designing of liturgy.

3. Encouraging the lay people and other clergy to take a part in worship.

4. Conducting worship so that parishioners are inspired to deepen their bond with God.

5. Making the ritual come alive so that lay people are motivated and empowered to serve God in the world.

Step Six—Gather Feedback

Each member of the committee should be assigned one or two categories on which to gather information and opinions from members of the congregation about the pastor's performance. For example, the committee will be interviewing people on the Vestry, people on church committees, new people on whom the pastor has made a call, students in courses taught by the pastor.

In some categories, members of the committee may need to interview clergy colleagues of the pastor and officials in your denomination or other people in the community.

If you decide to evaluate your pastor's counseling, it is not a good idea to ask for evaluation from the people the pastor has counseled. People the pastor has helped the most may have left in anger because the pastor refused to support their irresponsible behavior, and people who are pleased with the counseling may simply be those the pastor failed to challenge. Probably the only way to evaluate the pastor's counseling is to interview psycho-therapists to whom the pastor has made referrals.

Members of the committee may need to help people they are interviewing understand that the pastor has requested the evalua-tion and that the evaluation does not have any bearing on salary increases or the tenure of the pastor's appointment. The inter-viewer should make clear the purpose of the evaluation:

— to give the pastor a clear picture of how his work is per-ceived by the whole congregation.

— to share their insights with the pastor.

— to assist the pastor in developing a plan of continuing education and professional growth.

Here are some things to keep in mind while gathering information from the parish:

1. Be responsible for your category/criteria only.

2. In making contact with people, be sensitive to when, where, and how you will meet and talk. (Coffee hour is not ideal.)

3. Be sensitive to the people you pick to interview:

> a. You want to gain a good sense of the performance and how it affects each person you interview.
> b. You want to gain a good sense of what the strength is and what the weakness is.

4. Be sensitive to all points of view:
> a. You need people who can be honest in their perspective and who can be objective.
> b. Avoid people who you feel cannot give an adequate or fair assessment.

5. Don't take the evaluation with you if you go in person:
> a. Study and reflect on the content before you start.
> b. Internalize the category so you are familiar with it.
> c. Confidence in yourself and the task will help the people to be clear and trusting of you and the process.

6. Write up notes soon after your interview.

7. Be thoughtful about what is appropriate for your report.

8. Don't protect or withhold feedback because it may hurt. It is all valuable. You are asked to be responsible and honest to the task as well as sensitive to how the information is presented.

9. Be clear and open that you are helping in the pastor's continuing education and in supporting the pastor's ministry.

10. In every case, you will be asking, "What is your experience of the pastor?" In asking that question, you will need to:
> a. Get at each person's own feelings rather than how he or she feels it ought to be.
> b. Help people to be accurate—
> > Why is the response positive?
> > Why is the response negative?

c. Encourage:
1. Examples
2. Clarity
3. Honesty
d. Help people to be specific about their own experience and perception.
e. Assure them that the pastor is asking for and supporting this evaluation process.
f. Avoid and disregard statements such as:
"Everyone says"
"A lot of people are saying"

Step Seven—Prepare the Evaluation

This step is accomplished by the evaluation committee alone and it will take at least four hours. The person chairing the committee appoints one person to keep track of the scoring and another to record comments.

The time to be spent on each category is set based on the numerical weight you assigned to it. For example, if you assigned Worship a weight of 30, in a 4 hour meeting you would set aside 30% of 240 minutes, or 72 minutes, to discuss the pastor's performance in Worship. During this discussion the member of the committee assigned to that area will report the information and opinions collected. Each member of the committee will now privately assign a numerical score between 0 and 100 to each of the criteria under performance. Each of the members of the committee will then announce the scores they have individually given for each of the criteria, taking one criterion at a time.

In attempting to determine the final score for each of the criteria, the committee will have to listen to each other's reasons. For example, what specifically caused one person to give a 95 to "Preaching sermons that relate God's word to our lives" while another member of the committee rated the pastor's performance in that area only 65? The member of the committee appointed for the task will record comments made during this part of the evaluation. These comments should not appear in the report to the elected lay officials.

After arriving at a consensus for the score of each criterion under a category, the committee will then assign a score to the category as a whole. This need not be done with mathematical precision, but should reflect the consensus scores of the criteria with some attention paid to the relative importance of each. The committee needs to remember that their purpose is not to give a good score but to help the performance of the pastor. They are like a coach helping to improve the performance of the quarterback. Here is an example of scoring for one category:

Category: Worship	Category Score	91
		Scores
The best possible performance in worship will include:		
1. Preaching sermons that relate God's word to our lives.		94
2. Providing leadership and instruction in the designing of liturgy.		92
3. Encouraging the lay people and other clergy to take an active part in worship.		85
4. Conducting worship so that parishioners are inspired to deepen their bond with God.		92
5. Making the ritual come alive so that lay people are motivated and empowered to serve God in the world.		86
	Average	90

In the report that goes to the pastor, the committee will include relevant comments after each criteria. For example, the committee might explain that the pastor tries too hard to get all of the Bible lessons of the day into his sermons and sometimes confuses the people with too many ideas at once.

Also note that the category score in this example is not equal to a mathematical average. The committee felt more weight should be given to the pastor's obvious sincerity and devotion than to some of his shortcomings. In coming up with a number, however, the committee had to remember that their purpose was not to find a way to produce a higher score but to help the pastor improve the quality of ministry.

Each category is similarly scored, and then to determine the composite score for the evaluation, each category score is multiplied by the weight originally given. For example, if Worship were assigned a weight of 30, and the pastor were given a performance score of 91 in that area, his adjusted score would be 30% of 91 or 27.3. By adding up the adjusted scores the committee will arrive at the composite score for the evaluation of the pastor's performance.

The chairman and the two members appointed to keep track of the scores and the comments will prepare the final report to be reviewed by the committee at its next meeting.

When the report is adjusted to everyone's satisfaction, the chairman will see that the final report is reproduced in two versions: one with the specific comments for the use of the pastor and committee and one with the scores only for the elected lay officials.

The form to be used in reporting the evaluation might look like this. The blanks have been filled in only for those areas used in the previous examples. The total of the adjusted scores will produce the composite score for the evaluation.

EVALUATION

prepared for the Rev._____ Date _____

Category	Priority Weight	Assigned Score	Adjusted Score
A. _____	_____	_____	_____
B. Worship	30	91	27.30
C. _____			
D. Christian Education	11	85	9.35
E. Ministering	10	95	9.50
F. Counseling	9	82	7.38
G._____	_____	_____	_____
H. _____	_____	_____	_____
I. _____	_____	_____	_____
Totals - 100		xxx	

Step Eight—Report to the Pastor

In some ways this is the most important meeting in the process, and it can be the most uncomfortable for all concerned. The pastor is likely to approach the report of the committee with some apprehension. As much as most of us want a clear indication of how we are doing, we also have some fear of negative criticism because in a severe form such judgment can feel like condemnation. The committee may also experience some anxiety about giving the pastor their report. The last thing they want to do is to hurt the pastor's feelings and to risk damaging such an important relationship in their spiritual community. Many people find giving direct affirmation and praise equally difficult because it might make the pastor seem more separate and remote from ordinary people.

For the session to be useful, a climate of mutual trust is obviously necessary. That means a little time before the work begins should probably be devoted to catching up with each other by informal conversation, then silence to make the transition, and finally prayer that acknowledges mutual respect and asks for guidance.

To avoid misunderstanding, do not give the report to the pastor prior to the meeting. No one but the committee should see the report before it is handed to the pastor in person and explained to him.

— Allow at least 4 hours for this meeting. Divide the time as you did at the evaluation session allowing the same percent of your time for each category as you have assigned its weight. The chairman will be responsible for keeping the group on schedule.

— In each category, the members of the committee may add their comments to those in the written report as they explain their reasons for the scores. The numbers provide the occasion for this frank discussion. They are not an end in themselves.

— In each category, the pastor will ask questions for clarification and give personal responses to what the committee is reporting.

— As they move through the report, the committee and pastor together will identify areas where further training, continuing education, or changes in direction appear to be in order.

Step Nine—Provide Follow-up Support for the Pastor

At subsequent meetings the committee and pastor will outline objectives for the pastor's professional development in the next two years.

— Identify those areas where further training, continuing education, or changes seem to be in order.

— Establish objectives in each of these areas.

— Explore ways to meet these objectives. You cannot work out all of the details in one meeting, but you might have some specific recommendations at this time. For example, to work on the pastor's tendency to ignore other people's ideas and interests in worship, you might suggest that the pastor include a group of lay people in planning a series of worship services.

— Decide on the language and form you will use in reporting to the lay officials the objectives for the pastor's professional development that you will include with your report.

Step Ten—Report to the Elected Lay Officials

The chairman is responsible for getting written reports to all of the elected lay officials prior to the meeting at which the evaluation report is to be presented. Both the chairman and the pastor must be present at the meeting when the lay officials discuss the report. The oral presentation of the report should be brief, allowing time for questions and discussion.

Summary

Good luck. In some ways you have finished, in others you have just begun. If you need help call on us. Maybe we could give you some small bit of advice to speed you on your way.

> The Reverend James R. Adams, Rector
> St. Mark's Episcopal Church
> 118 3rd Street, SE
> Washington, D.C. 20003
> (202) 543-0053
>
> (Mrs.) Priscilla Adams
> 311 W. Myrtle Street
> Alexandria, Virginia 22301
> (703) 638-3218

In Summary

Congregations of all sizes and all shapes have successfully learned that evaluation can be a creative conversation between all involved in the leadership of the church. Designing an evaluation process that uniquely fits the needs of a pastor at a particular point in his or her ministry can be very helpful. Considering evaluation to be "mutual" so that all sharing in the tasks of the church can be included is beneficial to both the professional staff and the volunteer leadership of a congregation. Exciting and productive evaluation can occur—these churches prove that!

CHAPTER V

Denominations Can Help

Not only are pastors and congregations concerned about the effectiveness of ministry, so are denominations. Most have struggled with how to be helpful in assisting lay leaders and clergy in this important task. Judicatory offices often provide staff who are skilled in organizational development and can be of service in helping to design or lead an evaluation process. Many denominations have created elaborate processes which, although helpful in congregations with the time and talent to execute them, can appear so complex that they discourage some churches from pursuing them further. We will briefly consider three very different approaches to evaluation provided by the national offices of the United Methodist Church, the Evangelical Lutheran Church in America, and the Presbyterian Church (U.S.A.).

Methodists—A Covenantal Approach

Since 1968 the United Methodist Church has asked the Administrative Board of each church to evaluate the ministry of the congregation. In 1976 that process was broadened to include an evaluation of pastoral effectiveness as a companion to that of congregational effectiveness. That same year the district superintendent was to provide counsel and direct evaluation to each pastor as part of the D.S.'s supervision and feedback. Thus the Methodists have almost twenty years of experience in mutual evaluation that includes *both* the ministry of the pastor and that of the church as a whole.

Three manuals developed by the Division of Ordained Ministry of the General Board of Higher Education and Ministry of the United Methodist Church compose the basic process for mutual evaluation. All are introduced through the general theme "Developing and Evaluating an Effective Ministry—Colleagues in Dialogue." There are separate manuals for the administrative board, the pastor/staff relations committee, and pastors and diaconal ministers. These are based on the 1984 Book of Discipline of the United Methodist Church. The same theological foundation, evaluation theories, and suggested procedures and worksheets are used in all three manuals. The Reverend J. Richard Yeager was editor for each.

The *Manual for The Administrative Board* emphasizes eight concepts of evaluation—that it is a process, it receives information for decision making, it affirms strengths as well as identifies weaknesses, has statements that are specific and in commonly understood language, uses adverbs that describe behavior and don't pass judgment, assumes that evaluators are not experts, and does not evaluate everything every year. Over a three-year cycle an administrative board would evaluate "What a Congregation is Called to Be and Called to Do" based on eleven qualities and eleven ministries found in an additional pamphlet, "The Nature and Function of Effective Ministry."[1] This newly revised pamphlet adds three additional dimensions to the "to do" side of ministry and the earlier work can be easily adapted to accommodate these. The process includes a well-written timeline, worksheets for data gathering, and a suggested method of reporting back.

Beginning again with the theological principles of evaluation, the *Manual for Pastor/Staff Parish Relations Committee* moves quickly into the nature and purpose of professional staff evaluation. It provides a very sensitive exercise to prepare the pastor in light of the natural anxiety that occurs whenever one's performance is

being reviewed. Establishing a covenant for developing and evaluating a pastor's ministry is one recommendation as a beginning
point for establishing trust. A helpful section entitled "Some Clues
for Giving Feedback" enables all to feel effective and sensitive in
this stage of the process. Establishing priorities for the pastor's
ministry and reporting the decisions to the congregation rounds out
this well-written resource for pastoral review.

The Evangelical Lutheran Church in America— A Staff Support Committee

One of the first tasks of the newly formed Evangelical Lutheran
Church in America's Leadership Support Division for Ministry
was to provide a manual to assist in the personnel functions of the
congregation. The Rev. George Keck of Lutheran Theological
Seminary in Philadelphia was recruited to design and prepare the
manual and its suggested procedures. Each congregation is en-
couraged to have a Staff Support Committee who will deal with
the need for support of pastors and other staff, to clarify and com-
municate expectations, to manage conflict faithfully should it arise,
and to conduct annual reviews for all pastors employed by the
church. For each of these dynamics, a chapter lays out helpful
guidelines for responding to each need and decision point. Chapter
Six, "Continuing Education," is an excellent section on how the
pastor and committee might plan together for a meaningful educational experience. Extended study leaves (sabbaticals) are also
discussed including the benefits to the pastor and congregation and
how to address the unique requirements of planning for a pastor's
extended absence. Although the appendix contains suggestions
particularly useful for Lutherans, the "Reflections and Directions
Worksheet" provides thirty-six items clustered around five ministry functions that can be used as a simple evaluation tool by any
congregation.[2]

Presbyterians—Toward the Improvement of Ministry

The original work on the "Toward the Improvement of Ministry" pamphlets was done by the Vocation Agency of the former United Presbyterian Church in the U.S.A. in 1975. Now available through the Church Vocations Ministry Unit of the Presbyterian Church (U.S.A.), this series includes five booklets most recently revised in 1989. Each booklet can stand alone, but the pamphlets are designed to be used as a series. Two key components are *Pastoral Activities Index* and *Session Activities Index*. The *Pastoral Activities Index* is a detailed description of the activities in which pastors engage, organized into eight areas: worship, pastoral care, church education, mission interpretation, parish/community relationships, administration, relationships with judicatories, and ministry as a profession. *Session Activities Index* is organized in a similar manner with the seven major areas of the session's (local governing board) responsibilities in each. These areas are worship, pastoral care, church education, mission, governance, administration, and involvement with more inclusive judicatories. Both indexes were based on extensive research with Presbyterian pastors and elders on what constituted "competency" in these tasks of ministry. The introductions to each index emphasize the fact that ministry is relational as well as functional. The user is cautioned not to confuse the performance of ministerial tasks with the vocation of ministry. The third booklet in the series, *Planning for Ministry* uses the extensive indexes to assist the session and staff in establishing priorities for the congregation's life and work, the session's work, and the pastor's work. The process acknowledges that these priorities do not always need to match identically and that priorities are generally best established for manageable periods of time rather than indefinitely.

The two booklets in the series most relevant to our discussion are *Pastoral Performance Profile* and *Guidelines for a Session Personnel Committee*. The latter covers the importance of clear and updated job descriptions, the need for goals and objectives, a sample review process, and counsels that reviews of compensation should be separate from performance reviews. It is a helpful guide for the lay leader elected to this committee. The *Pastoral Performance Profile* is a pastor-directed comprehensive review process requiring approximately fifteen contact hours.

Use of the *Pastoral Performance Profile* involves the pastor selecting a peer pastor and one member of the congregation whom he or she trusts to give honest assessment. After familiarizing themselves with the twenty-eight scales of the *Pastoral Activities Index*, the feedback team agrees on what determines "highly competent," "acceptable," and "below standard" evaluation on the performance of each. The booklet presents each scale with a definition, (example: Scale #3—Sermon Preparation. From the definition: A. Prepares sermons from a limited variety of the books of the Bible; uses some references and theological insights; usually spends adequate time in preparation.), a rationale (example: One of the significant factors in the pastor's ministry is the quality of sermons presented.), what the highly competent pastor does (example: In preparing sermons, the pastor places a high priority on time needed for preparation, devoting prime time for prayer and study.) and performance information needed by the review team (example: Resource materials used, including Confessions of the church).[3] The review team then collects and summarizes data on the scales, recognizing that no pastor is going to do everything equally well. The gathered data is then shared with the pastor and a plan entitled "Steps Toward Increased Competency" is completed. This is a rather complex form of evaluation. For those interested in a simpler strategy, the materials can be adapted for a less demanding process. This Presbyterian approach, which includes a peer review, may be blended with another peer supervision process designed by Deborah and Michael Jinkins, Presbyterian ministers writing for *Action Information* in 1986. They suggest a design that includes planning, a period of "observation" where the team takes detailed note of how a pastor functions in visible situations, and then a feedback conference.[4] This addition of verbatim feedback may be a helpful strengthening of the "Toward the Improvement of Ministry" procedure.

In Summary

Most denominations are concerned about regular review of the ministry of the congregation and that of the pastor. Resources have been developed to assist in the evaluation process, and judicatory staff may be available to help implement it. Many of these resources involve the use of data gathering and diagnostic instruments. Congregations using these materials may need to adapt them to fit the needs and time constraints of their particular situations.

CHAPTER VI

A Dozen Reminders

By now I hope the reader is convinced that review and evaluation do not need to be feared. In fact, used with care and sensitivity, evaluation can strengthen all aspects of ministry and may even save a tenuous relationship between pastor and parish by addressing needs before they become issues. We have identified the benefits of evaluation for both minister and congregation. We have grounded our approach to evaluation in a theological context. Having examined the potential problems in such reviews, we have strategized to avoid them. The success stories of four different congregations have been presented. The materials offered by several denominations have added even more options to consider. This last chapter now sums up the key learning in this exploration. What *really* works and what should we keep before us as we plan for ministry review?

A Dozen Reminders

1. Evaluation and review are most effective when congregation and pastor are engaged in a mutual process. Ministry belongs to the whole people of God and not just the pastor. Therefore the ministry of the congregation requires regular evaluation just as the minister's does.

2. Evaluations work best when they are part of a regularly

scheduled process of measuring effectiveness. Some method of reviewing the goals and objectives of a congregation's mission and of a pastor's work should be conducted annually. When discussion and feedback are expected as a normal part of life together the anxiety about such examination is greatly reduced.

3. Comprehensive reviews of a pastor's performance are not helpful when major conflicts are present. Using evaluation as a weapon against a pastor is never acceptable. When regular review is a part of a congregation and pastor's life together, problems can be identified much earlier. The time to begin a review process is *not* when the relationship is already in trouble!

4. Keep it simple! The more complex an evaluation process becomes the more likely participation in it will be limited, the process may not be completed, or it will result in a very large detailed report never to be heard from again! This is why it may be best to measure only a few aspects of ministry at a time rather than the entire efforts of a pastor and a congregation.

5. There are particular times when special reviews can be helpful. During a minister's first year of service, quarterly conversations with a six-month and one-year evaluation and renegotiation can assist the new pastor and the governing board to keep on track with mutual goals. We've discovered that a more comprehensive review every four to five years can be of immense value in a longer pastorate. Many clergy can acquire excellent insights through a mid-career and pre-retirement visit to a career counseling center in conjunction with more comprehensive reviews.

6. Compensation reviews for ministers should not be held in conjunction with performance reviews. When a person's livelihood is tied to how well he or she is perceived to be functioning in a particular position, the stakes on the review are immediately escalated. This quite often blocks honest reflection and assessment and encourages the clergyperson and all those supportive of him or her to present the most positive picture possible. The creative examination of what needs to be improved, done differently, added, or eliminated is hampered. Many congregations find that performance reviews in the fall and compensation reviews in the spring can avoid much of this tension.

7. Comprehensive evaluation of a pastor is most helpful when the minister requests it. Major reviews that focus intensely on particular aspects of a pastor's performance can be extremely helpful when the pastor desires such feedback. Planning the process in such a way that the pastor being reviewed can contribute to the design also leads to ownership on the part of all. When a minister considers the evaluation something to "be endured" rather than a helpful tool for personal and professional growth, you can expect the results to be less than satisfying.

8. A design that is tailor-made to fit the particular situation is often better than a packaged process. Because there are many factors affecting a congregation (size, history, finances, location, theological perspective, etc.) and a pastor (years of experience, length of service, health, particular gifts, etc.), no single plan for evaluation may necessarily fit. Therefore it is often advisable to adapt existing models or design one's own to meet the needs for meaningful evaluation.

9. An outside consultant can be of assistance. Professionals in the organizational development or personnel fields can be useful in many instances. Contracting with a person outside the congregation can lend a professional tone to the process and provide a certain objectivity. Many denominations provide such individuals in the form of judicatory staff. Sometimes a particularly skilled pastor in a neighboring congregation can be of assistance. One word of caution: Denominational staff and even colleagues in ministry do bring a perspective on the church and the pastor based on previous contact. Although most will attempt to set any bias aside, carefully discussing these assumptions can go far in eliminating unacknowledged agendas. When using a professional in evaluation it is important to get references from other churches or not-for-profit organizations that have used his or her services. The match between consultant and client is extremely important for the establishment of trust and rapport. If at all possible, contract with the consultant for the entire process including the report and follow-up. This provides overall assistance in designing the evaluation, gathering and interpreting data, decision making for change or new priorities, a report out process, and monitoring the follow-up.

10. Focus on positives as well as negatives. It is as important to identify what a congregation and a pastor are doing *well* as it is to discover what is not going well. Evaluations that simply seek to name what should happen differently or not at all provide an unbalanced perspective on the overall picture of ministry. Individuals need to be reminded that "evaluation" means just that—a careful appraisal and study. Knowledge of things that are actually working well gives needed emotional support to those areas that may need special attention in the future.

11. Be clear from the beginning what will happen as a result of the evaluation. Who will see the findings? How will a report to the congregation be made? If changes in job descriptions or mission goals are to be made, who will make them? Then be certain these things do happen. Nothing feels worse than to be part of a process and never know what happened as a result of it. Again, evaluation should never be used as a way of getting rid of a pastor. If the problems are that serious, a conflict consultant is needed—not a pastoral review!

12. Provide a system for monitoring decisions. When changes are proposed in either the direction of a congregation's efforts or in the pastor's performance, they need to be supported and monitored. Timelines, measurable goals and strategies, and "temperature taking" sessions can all be helpful ways of sustaining the learning from an evaluation. If the evaluation has been part of a yearly process, this will most likely occur as a mid-year review of how things are going. A personnel committee or pastor/parish relations committee should be monitoring progress if the changes are related to the pastor's regular work. However, when the learning from a more comprehensive review indicates *significant* change or redirection the conversations and support need to be more intentional. Mutual accountability and a periodic check on "how we're doing" can go a long way in assuring that the decided upon changes will occur.

In Conclusion

Please remember that whatever process you use, whoever is affected by the outcome, however long or short your timetable—you are not in this process alone. Christ, who is the true head of the church, is our constant companion in the journey. When we take seriously our call as Christians to share in a common ministry, we agree to be open to the leading of God's Spirit. The hard job of evaluation is part of that commitment. As you approach this task, be challenged by the words of Paul to the Corinthians, "Keep alert, stand firm in your faith, be courageous, be strong. Let all that you do be done in love."[1]

NOTES

Chapter 1

1. C. Ellis Nelson, *Using Evaluation in Theological Education* (Nashville: Discipleship Resources, 1975), 39.

2. Loren B. Mead, *Evaluation Of, By, For and To the Clergy* (Washington, DC: The Alban Institute, 1977), 15.

3. Daniel V. Biles, *Pursuing Excellence in Ministry* (Washington, DC: The Alban Institute, 1988), 9.

4. Richard Ullman, "Taking Stock of Our Ministry," *Action Information* Vol. X: No. 2, May-June 1984 (Washington, DC: The Alban Institute).

5. Donald Hagerty, Jr., "Evaluating Clergy Peformance," *Christian Ministry* (January, 1983).

Chapter 2

1. "All the Live Long Day: Women and Work," a study paper of the Presbyterian Church (U.S.A.), 1988.

2. "Theological and Theoretical Foundations for Evaluating Ministry," a pamphlet prepared by the Division of Ordained Ministry, Board of Higher Education and Ministry of the United Methodist Church (Nashville, 1990).

3. Ibid.

4. Paul Dietterich and Russell Wilson, *An Experiment in District Revitalization #4 —A Process of Local Church Vitalization* (Naperville, IL: Center for Parish Development, 1976), 67.

5. Roy Oswald, "Getting a Fix on Your Ministry," an On Demand Publication (Washington, DC: The Alban Institute), 9.

6. George Keck, *Staff Support Committee: A Vision for Mutual Ministry* (Chicago: Evangelical Lutheran Church in America, 1988), 5.

Chapter III

1. Douglas A. Walrath, *Planning for Your Church* (Philadelphia: The Westminster Press, 1984), 33.
2. Lyle E. Schaller, *Create Your Own Future!* (Nashville: Abingdon Press, 1991), 58.
3. "Theological and Theoretical Foundations for Evaluating Ministry," Op. Cit., 2.
4. Roy Oswald, Interview at Estes Park, Colorado in July, 1991.
5. Nelson, Op.Cit., 34, United Methodist Church, 1975, pg. 34
6. Diane Fassel, Presentation at meeting of Women Church Executives, Presbyterian Church (U.S.A.), St. Louis, MO, 1986.
7. Roy Oswald, "Alban Institute Approaches to Assessment," *Clergy Assessment and Career Development*, Richard A. Hunt, John E. Hinkle, Jr. and H. Newton Malony, editors (Nashville: Abington, 1990), 180.

Chapter IV

1. Catherine Holmes Clark, "Annual Church Review Procedure," an On Demand Publication (Washington, DC: The Alban Institute).
2. Process designed by Dr. Wynette Barnard, Manager of National Programs for Resource Careers, Cleveland, Ohio. Used with permission.

Chapter V

1. "The Nature and Function of Effective Ministry", a pamphlet prepared by the Division of Ordained Ministry, Board of Higher Education and Ministry, the United Methodist Church (Nashville, 1984).
2. George Keck, *Staff Support Committee: A Vision for Mutual Ministry* (Chicago: Division for Ministry, Evangelical Lutheran Church in America, 1988).
3. "Toward the Improvment of Ministry," a series of pamphlets produced by the Church Vocations Unit (formerly Vocation Agency) of the Presbyterian Church (U.S.A.), 1984-89.
4. Deborah and Michael Jinkins, "Increasing Competence in

Ministry with Collegial Supervision," *Action Information* Vol. XII: No. 6, November-December, 1986 (Washington, DC: The Alban Institute).

Chapter VI

1. New Revised Standard Version of the Holy Bible (Division of Christian Education, National Council of Churches, 1989).

BIBLIOGRAPHY

"All the Live Long Day: Women and Work," a study paper of the
Presbyterian Church (U.S.A.), 1988.

Biles, Daniel V. *Pursuing Excellence in Ministry.* Washington, DC:
The Alban Institute, 1988.

Clark, Catherine Holmes. "Annual Church Review Procedure," an
On Demand Publication. Washington, DC: The Alban
Institute.

Dietterich, Paul and Wilson, Russell. *An Experiment in District
Revitalization #4 — A Process of Local Church Vitalization.*
Naperville, IL: Center for Parish Development, 1976.

Hagerty, Donald, Jr. "Evaluating Clergy Performance." *Christian
Ministry*, January, 1983.

Keck, George. *Staff Support Committee: A Vision for Mutual Ministry.*
Chicago: Evangelical Lutheran Church in America, 1988.

Mead, Loren. *Evaluation Of, By, For and To the Clergy.* Washington,
DC: The Alban Institute, 1977.

"The Nature and Function of Effective Ministry," a pamphlet prepared by
the Division of Ordained Ministry, Board of Higher Education and
Ministry, the United Methodist Church. Nashville, 1984.

Nelson, C. Ellis. *Using Evaluation in Theological Education.* Nashville: Discipleship Resources, 1975.

Oswald, Roy. "Alban Institute Approaches to Assessment." *Clergy Assessment and Career Development.* Nashville: Abington, 1990.

Oswald, Roy. "Getting a Fix on Your Ministry," an On Demand Publication. Washington, DC: The Alban Institute.

Schaller, Lyle E. *Create Your Own Future!* Nashville: Abingdon, 1991.

"Theological and Theoretical Foundations for Evaluating Ministry," a pamphlet prepared by the Division of Ordained Ministry, Board of Higher Education and Ministry of the United Methodist Church. Nashville, 1990.

"Toward the Improvement of Ministry," a series of pamphlets produced by the Church Vocations Unit (formerly Vocation Agency) of the Presbyterian Church (U.S.A.), 1984-1989.

Ullman, Richard. "Taking Stock of Our Ministry," *Action Information,* Vol. X: No. 2, 1984. Washington, DC: The Alban Institute.

Walrath, Douglas. *Planning for Your Church.* Philadelphia: Westminster Press, 1984.

Welcome to the work of Alban Institute...
the leading publisher and congregational
resource organization for clergy and laity today.

Your purchase of this book means you have an interest in the kinds of information, research, consulting, networking opportunities and educational seminars that Alban Institute produces and provides. We are a non-denominational, non-profit 25-year-old membership organization dedicated to providing practical and useful support to religious congregations and those who participate in and lead them.

Alban is acknowledged as a pioneer in learning and teaching on *Conflict Management *Faith and Money *Congregational Growth and Change *Leadership Development *Mission and Planning *Clergy Recruitment and Training *Clergy Support, Self-Care and Transition *Spirituality and Faith Development *Congregational Security.

Our membership is comprised of over 8,000 clergy, lay leaders, congregations and institutions who benefit from:
- ❖ 15% discount on hundreds of Alban books
- ❖ $50 per-course tuition discount on education seminars
- ❖ Subscription to *Congregations*, the Alban journal (a $30 value)
- ❖ Access to Alban research and (soon) the "Members-Only" archival section of our web site www.alban.org

For more information on Alban membership or to be added to our catalog mailing list, call 1-800-486-1318, ext.243 or return this form.

Name and Title: _____

Congregation/Organization: _____

Address: _____

City: _____ Tel.: _____

State: _____ Zip: _____ Email: _____

BKIN

The Alban Institute
Attn: Membership Dept.
7315 Wisconsin Avenue
Suite 1250 West
Bethesda, MD 20814-3211